FOR AUTISM FRIENDLY WORKPLACES

100 Lessons
for
Employers and Employees
to Succeed Together

Patty Pacelli
GrowingUpAutistic.com

Six-Word Lessons for Autism Friendly Workplaces – 6wordlessons.com

Copyright © 2014 by Patty Pacelli

Published by Pacelli Publishing
9905 Lake Washington Blvd. NE, #D-103
Bellevue, Washington 98004
Pacellipublishing.com

ISBN-10: 1-933750-38-3
ISBN-13: 978-1-933750-38-5

Introduction

Our second child Trevor was born in December of 1992, and diagnosed with PDD-NOS (Pervasive Development Disorder-Not Otherwise Specified) while in kindergarten. We learned about autism throughout his childhood, and relied on our public school's teachers, counselors and specialists, whom I see as true heroes. There were challenges along the way, and we learned as much as we could. Trevor graduated from high school right on schedule with a B average. It was a proud, exciting time, but in some ways even more of an "unknown" than when he was diagnosed with autism in kindergarten.

Now that he is in college, I am writing this book to help build awareness that as children with autism become adults, they need to live independently and support themselves with meaningful work, a dream that all parents have for their kids. This book is for individuals with autism either looking for jobs or currently working, and for employers, human resource managers, small business owners, supervisors and co-workers of adults with autism.

This book contains 100 short lessons to give both employees and employers guidelines on helping adults with autism find careers that fulfill and support them, and thrive in the workplace while benefiting their employers with their skills and talents. I hope this helps many adults with autism and employers to find well-fitting, meaningful and productive working relationships.

Acknowledgements

Thank-you to the experts in the field of autism and employment who so willingly met with me and shared their knowledge and opinions: Kim Kimbell, Sara Gardner, Lisa Iland Hilbert, Manfred Seidler, Michael Goodwill, Garry Burge, Ben Wilshire and Elaine Duncan.

I am grateful to the board members of the Seattle Children's Autism Guild for their continual interest and support. They have inspired and encouraged me to help young adults with autism find fulfilling careers: Andrea Duffield, Karen Kaizuka, Susan Steckler, Elijah Winfrey, Lisa Iland Hilbert and Julie O'Brien. Thanks also to Seattle Children's Autism Center representatives, Katrina Davis, Megen Strand and Tammy Mitchel for direction, ideas and support.

I also appreciate the help and information from Paige Morrow of Extraordinary Ventures and Jeri Kendle of the Southwest Autism Research & Resource Center. Both of these organizations are doing exciting things to help adults with autism find meaningful work.

I dedicate this book to my husband Lonnie, who first had the idea of the "autism friendly workplace," my daughter Briana, who was and still is the best big sister anyone with autism could have, and for Trevor, who has amazed us with his accomplishments and growth, and continues the fight to live and succeed in a different, difficult world.

Terminology

While working on this book, I heard about an opinion in the autism and disability community that disabilities should be referred to in "person first" language, i.e., "person with autism" rather than "autistic person."

I did a survey on the subject on our Growing Up Autistic Facebook page and received comments that were split about fifty/fifty on which way they preferred, and some said it didn't matter.

Because of my survey results, and my own opinion as a parent and writer, I have chosen to use both terms in this book, partially because of grammar and word count considerations. I hope the choice of wording will not affect the message and intent of the book, and that these differences of opinion will not divide a community that should be working together to support all individuals with disabilities.

Table of Contents

The Need for Autism Friendly Workplaces

1

Traits of autism hinder job possibilities.

My son Trevor applied for dozens of summer jobs during his high school and college years. He was occasionally called for interviews, but never got the jobs, largely because of his autism. Eventually, he found two summer jobs, and his work was stellar. I hope to help other young adults find meaningful employment.

2

Children with autism quickly become adults.

Research is clear that the number of children being diagnosed with autism is rising. The maturing of these children will lead to more adults entering the workforce in the coming years. This book is a springboard for how companies and the autism community can work together to hire these individuals, resulting in productivity and success for all.

3

Employment statistics can be quite discouraging.

For autistic adults aged 21-25, app-roximately one-half (53.4%) with an autism spectrum disorder have ever worked for pay outside the home since leaving high school, according to a 2013 study from the *Journal of the American Academy of Child & Adolescent Psychiatry* (jaacap.com) by Dr. Paul Shattuck and his team.

4

Autism employment is lowest among disabilities.

In a national study of young adults who had received any type of special services in high school, the adults with autism spectrum disorders (ASDs) had the lowest employment rate of all other disabilities. The study concluded that there is a particular difficulty with finding work for the autistic population. (jaacap.com)

5

Pay for autistic workers is low.

Adults with autism typically earn less than others in the workforce. In addition, studies show that autistic employees are limited to fewer occupational types. Dr. Shattuck's study also found that conversational abilities and higher household income result in higher-paying jobs. (jaacap.com)

6

Work is a basic human need.

Human beings were made to work, and adults with autism are no different. Employment leads to a better mood, higher self-esteem, and improved physical health; and it allows autistic adults to further develop their skills and understanding. Our son Trevor liked being around people and enjoyed the feeling of accomplishment at his jobs.

7

More barriers exist for autistic employees.

Individuals with autism experience additional hindrances in finding and retaining jobs. A 2013 article by Tamar Najarian lists these barriers as: sensory overload issues; problems showing emotions; inadequate language; social awkwardness; inability to handle large crowds; need for things to be a certain way; and lack of proper mental transition into adulthood. (emaxhealth.com)

Career Preparation for Parents and Children

8

Start early and involve the family.

Parents should begin thinking about employment for children with autism when they are young. Involving them in household chores, volunteer work, and other projects will prepare them for employment, says Michael Goodwill, manager of transition services at PROVAIL in Seattle. From a young age, Trevor did weekly chores and took care of his own needs as much as possible.

9

Plan for employment in elementary school.

Career planning can start as soon as children begin developing interests, at age 14 or sooner, say transition specialists. Taking note of interests, especially their passions, can help them pursue and cultivate them. If they talk about dreams that seem unrealistic, encourage them anyway. Trevor told us at age 9 that he wanted to be a movie director; he is now 21 and studying film at a university.

10

Teach early independence for later rewards.

When raising Trevor, we always hoped that he would be able to live on his own when he grew up. Because he is high functioning, and because we worked toward that goal from his childhood, he is now living in a university residence hall, a great step toward the next goal of paid employment to support himself and continue living on his own.

11

Independent living can increase employment rate.

The goal of independent living is important, and studies have shown that it leads to great employment success. "Autistic individuals are six times more likely to find and retain a job if they live alone or with a partner, run a household, and have previously held any job for longer than six months," according to emaxhealth.com.

12

Find out about skills and preferences.

Autistic children should job-shadow as early as middle school, and look for job sampling opportunities, volunteering and internships, to learn about various work environments. They should also cultivate life skills such as traveling and using public transportation. (*Life Journey Through Autism: a Guide to Transition to Adulthood*, OAR and SARRC)

13

Try to see challenges as strengths.

While watching for strengths, be aware of subject areas or tasks that are challenging or difficult for your child. Keep them in mind when envisioning the future, but consider how a challenge at home could be a strength in the workplace. Trevor was hypersensitive about being on time, which caused conflicts with the family occasionally, but it became a strength when he had his first job.

How to Find the Best Jobs

14

School-to-work programs foster success.

School-to-work programs are government-funded programs that give students with disabilities opportunities to work with contracted employment agencies who match company job openings to student workers. Students can participate in these programs while in high school, or directly after high school, as part of a school district transition program.

26

15

Transition programs lead to successful employment.

Transition programs that guide students from high school to the workplace are "tremendously successful" in King County, Washington, according to Goodwill. His agency, PROVAIL, saw 60 to 70 percent of students in their school-to-work program find jobs in the past year.

16

Transition specialists and businesses work together.

Businesses are usually very receptive to hiring employees with disabilities, according to Goodwill. He said they often create specific jobs to fit employees and hire them for the times and hours they are available. As long as companies have the right information, they are usually happy to hire individuals with disabilities.

17

Know that being older has advantages.

Autistic adults "who are older, come from households of higher income, and are higher functioning in society" are more likely to find jobs, according to emaxhealth.com. It's harder for young adults with autism to transition to adulthood in general, so this also makes it difficult to retain employment.

18

Alternative methods may lead to employment.

Along with early preparation at home, and transition and school-to-work programs, Elaine Duncan, a psychotherapist who works with adults with autism, suggests that a great way for those on the spectrum to find jobs is to use "back door methods," such as advocates and any acquaintances who can help them network and lead them to the right jobs.

19

Employees should agree with company values.

Because people with autism are more "black and white" in their thinking, and usually have strong opinions and beliefs, it's very important that their values align with their company's values, according to Duncan. If they have a strong positive opinion about a company's core philosophy, they will be happier and more productive working for that company.

20

Ideal employment opportunities usually involve independence.

People with autism are usually not highly team-oriented, and prefer to be on their own, and Duncan finds that the vast majority of her clients find work in the computer industry. She has also found that individuals with autism are successful as tutors, because they enjoy using their intelligence and expertise while working one-on-one with students.

21

Many fields are compatible for autism.

Emaxhealth.com recommends jobs in the information technology field, among others. They suggest computer programmer, engineer, drafter, commercial artist, photographer, graphic designer, web designer, cartoonist, librarian, mechanic, craftsman, technical repairman, carpenter, welder, building maintenance, accountant, statistician, and journalist as good jobs for those with autism.

22

There are jobs for nonverbal employees.

Jobs for nonverbal or nonspeaking autistic adults include janitor, store stocker, library helper, factory assembly worker, copy shop helper, warehouse helper, landscaping, data entry, and office helper. Any job that doesn't require communicating verbally with others is a possibility. (emaxhealth.com)

23

It's OK to avoid some jobs.

While everyone is different, there are some jobs that are simply not suitable for most people with autism. Emaxhealth.com lists these jobs to avoid: cashier, waiter/waitress, casino dealer, taxi dispatcher, ticket agent, market trader, auctioneer, receptionist, and most customer service jobs.

24

Family businesses offer alternative work opportunities.

For a different approach from traditional job-hunting, creative parents can help their children with autism find appropriate jobs by starting businesses that will capitalize on their child's strengths, and possibly train them to eventually take over the business and run it on their own or with help from other employees.

25

Starting a new business channels enthusiasm.

Autistic individuals should consider starting a business, because autistic people "have so much drive, enthusiasm and intelligence," Duncan says, so it's nice to channel that into a business venture. It "gets them out of that box they don't fit into." She said, "Doing something original allows them to thrive with their differences.

26

Joining with others can create opportunities.

A group of parents in Chapel Hill, North Carolina created several small businesses to provide employment for their children with autism. Their nonprofit, Extraordinary Ventures, employs over 40 adults with autism and other disabilities in their own event center. Workers do laundry, make candles, and many other tasks. (extraordinaryventures.org)

27

Training programs exist for autistic adults.

Southwest Autism Research & Resource Center has a program called Culinary-Works (culinaryworks.com) that teaches cooking and food service skills to adults with autism, then helps them launch careers by arranging internships or jobs at their own coffee shops and catering companies. SARRC has placed over 75 students in job positions.

28

Good training can lead to entrepreneurship.

A student in Arizona's CulinaryWorks program completed specialized training, interned at a bakery, took private lessons with a pastry chef, and has now launched his own business. Because of help from a local autism center and other volunteers and businesses willing to get involved, this adult on the autism spectrum is self-employed and supporting himself.

29

Many companies have disability hiring programs.

It is not uncommon for large companies to specifically focus on hiring certain numbers of employees with disabilities, according to Goodwill. Companies value these employees' talents and want to be more diverse by employing all types of people. Many of these jobs are high-paying, professional jobs with good career potential.

ADA Laws and Rules for Work

30

All parties must understand discrimination laws.

The Americans with Disabilities Act (ADA), enacted in 1990, states in the Title I employment section that qualified app-licants with disabilities may not be discriminated against in application procedures, hiring, advancement and discharge, workers compensation, job training and other terms and privileges of employment. (U.S. Department of Labor)

31

Discrimination can surface in various forms.

Title I of the ADA says that discrimination may include limiting or classifying an applicant or employee in an adverse way, denying employment to someone who is qualified, not making reasonable accommodations, or not advancing employees with disabilities. Knowing these rights ensures that everyone is treated fairly. (U.S. Department of Labor)

32

Understand the Section 503 Rehabilitation Act.

Section 503, from 1973, adds more specific rules about employers with federal contracts or subcontracts. If contracts are more than $10,000, employers must take affirmative action to hire, retain and promote qualified individuals with disabilities. Those seeking employment should be aware of this provision. (U.S. Department of Labor)

33

503 changes will provide more benefits.

Section 503 is undergoing updates that should benefit employees with disabilities. The new law will explicitly require nondiscrimination and affirmative action. Also, the definition of a "qualified individual with a disability" will be broadened to someone "unable to perform a major life activity that the average person can perform," which would include job duties. (U.S. Department of Labor)

34

Interviewees need not address medical issues.

Applicants with autism should keep in mind that the changes in the 503 law will prohibit any medical inquiries before making an offer. Employers may only ask about abilities to perform job-related functions. Medical exams or inquiries will only be permitted if "job related and consistent with business necessity." (U.S. Department of Labor)

Best Interview Practices for the Employer

35

Treat autistic people like anyone else.

Employers are not allowed to ask an interviewee about a disability, or even treat him like he has a disability, says human resources consultant Kim Kimbell. Employers may only ask the interviewee if he is able to perform the functions of the job. Disclosing the disability is up to the prospective employee, but he certainly does not have to do so during the interview.

36

Always look for the best fit.

Consider where people with autism will fit best, says Duncan, a former recruiter who now counsels adults on the spectrum. They should be placed in jobs with the appropriate co-workers, environments and job duties. People will be happiest and most productive in jobs for which they are well-suited.

37

Let the applicant show his skills.

An autistic person can often most effectively show his skills through a sample activity, such as proofing a sample document for an editing position. This can help employers make more accurate hiring decisions. It can be difficult for autistic people to "sell themselves" and put their skills and attributes into words, even if they are excellent candidates.

Interview Tips for People with Autism

38

Consider working with an interview coach.

Interview coaches can coordinate with employers to get questions in advance, and coach interviewees in the actual interview space. This has made a significant difference in helping applicants feel prepared for interviews, says Lisa Iland Hilbert of Social Bridge, which provides interview coaching. Coaches give interviewees lists of topics to avoid and points to highlight when interviewing.

39

Memorize and use an elevator pitch.

People with autism often have good memorizing skills, according to Hilbert, who works with autistic adults. It's easy for them to prepare a 30-second "elevator pitch," to tell prospective employers about their talents, skills, experience and abilities, and why they are best for the job. They should prepare answers for questions such as, "Tell us about yourself," and "Why do you want this job?"

40

Prepare something unique for the interview.

If autistic applicants can give a prospective employer a method for demonstrating his skills that is more creative than describing them verbally, it will help the employer to better identify his abilities. Hilbert suggests applicants prepare video clips, websites or portfolios of work relevant to the position to more easily show their skills.

41

Don't talk about autism during interview.

As discussed earlier, applicants with autism do not have to disclose any disabilities at the interview. They should learn the questions that interviewers are not allowed to ask, and only talk about their job qualifications. Sara Gardner, program manager of Autism Spectrum Navigators at Bellevue College says, "Wait until you get the job to disclose."

42

Exceptions to nondisclosure at the interview.

One reason to disclose autism during an interview would be when someone simply "doesn't present well," said Duncan, because of differences in communication and social skills. Disclosing autism might help the interviewer understand the reason for lower than average social skills, allowing the interviewer to focus on the skills necessary to do the job.

Reasonable Accommodations for Employers to Offer

43

Accommodations help employer and employee succeed.

In the ideal scenario, giving autistic employees accommodations would help the company run more effectively while helping autistic employees to be productive, leading to better products or services and more profit. All parties should work together to allow autistic employees to be productive without sacrificing the work environment for others.

44

Options for accommodations make a difference.

All onboarding employees should be given a survey or menu of options, suggests Hilbert, asking their preferences for things like sound, light, physical work space, type of communication desired, methods for performance appraisals and more. This allows autistic employees to simply state their preferences along with everyone else, without feeling different or singled out.

45

Workplace design can work for everyone.

The concept of "Universal Design" makes workplaces comfortable and accommodating for those with autism as well as those with other disabilities, while not infringing on employees without disabilities, Gardner said. This format makes it easy for people with autism to fit in to the work environment and do their jobs in the most productive way possible.

46

Step-by-step instructions ensure clarity.

People with autism need clear, step-by-step instructions so they know exactly what is expected of them, along with very detailed job descriptions they can refer to often. They are not less intelligent; they just process differently and are often visual learners, so the more clearly directions are spelled out, the better they will be at following those directions.

47

More showing than telling is effective.

Trevor's supervisor at his maintenance job, Manfred Seidler, observed that Trevor learned better by being shown how to do something, rather than just told verbally. When he showed Trevor how to lock up all the doors in the building, he physically walked through the locations with him, and after one time, "he got it," and never forgot the process.

48

Visual tools make a big difference.

Anything that is more visual and demonstrative will help autistic employees better understand what is expected of them on the job. Trevor said that calendars with deadlines were especially beneficial to him. Videos and slide shows are also helpful ways to teach an autistic person, rather than simply giving verbal instructions.

49

Accommodate sensory issues to reduce overload.

Many autistic people have physical sensitivities that can make workplaces difficult. Sara Gardner, who has sensory processing differences, has difficulty with bright lights, as well as office sounds such as typing, so she has arranged for the overhead lights in her office to be turned off, and often wears earplugs on the job.

50

Autistic workers need more private space.

It can be helpful for those with autism to work behind a closed door, even for part of the day. Sara Gardner has an accommodation for her office mate to work elsewhere for part of each day; a conference room could also meet this need. Because this can come across as rude or standoffish, managers should educate all employees to show tolerance and understanding.

51

Quiet surroundings lead to better focus.

While everyone is different, most people with autism spectrum disorders have some type of sensitivity to sound, even soft, continuous sounds, such as typing. Duncan says even road noise, fans and conversations can "drive them crazy because they can't filter out sounds like other people." They can get headaches and lose focus from these sounds. Ear protection can help.

52

All employees should respect others' differences.

Although an autistic employee may be allowed to wear headphones while he works, Gardner notes that this can send a social cue that she doesn't want to talk or socialize, so she could be considered rude, unsociable, or not team-oriented. Managers can encourage tolerance and open communication among all.

69

53

Loud music can be especially distressing.

People with autism can be very sensitive to loud music playing in the background, whether in a retail store, restaurant, warehouse or office. Public or work spaces would be more autism-friendly if they played the music low enough for people to talk, which would be appreciated by not only employees, but any customers with autism as well.

54

Working location can make or break.

Even if they aren't bothered by noise, autistic employees often work best when they have a dedicated space that isn't too close to other people. Hilbert suggested sitting on the outer edge of a group of office cubicles, or in a separate area, toward the edge of a larger area or manufacturing floor. Working farther away from coffee and lunch break areas is usually helpful, too, to keep from distractions.

55

Regular risk assessments keep everyone safe.

Garry Burge, an adult with Asperger's and an advocate for working adults on the spectrum, says that when autistic employees are working with machinery and equipment, there should be regular risk assessments and check-ins to make sure they are using the equipment properly and being safe.

56

Employees need guidance in question protocol.

Some adults on the spectrum need guidance to ask questions or get clarification, according to Hilbert. Some are hesitant to ask, while others ask too frequently. Creating a flowchart illus-trating the types of questions appropriate for HR, supervisor, job coach, or colleague, can help employees direct questions appropriately.

57

Provide a predictable framework for feedback.

While autistic employees need to get used to the culture of feedback, Hilbert said they also can benefit from the structure of knowing that it will be given at an expected time, place and method. Something like a weekly check-in, with both positive feedback as well as suggestions, given at the same time and place, is a good way to approach performance appraisals.

58

Advanced notice of recognition is helpful.

While most employees love to have a surprise award or kudos given, those on the spectrum would prefer to know ahead of time that they will be recognized. They will appreciate advanced notice of any type of event to recognize or thank them or others, especially if it will interrupt their usual workday routine.

59

One-on-one settings maximize learning.

When learning something new, Hilbert says that many times autistic employees "need more one-on-one attention," rather than being taught as part of a group. This is because of the differences in processing, and the sensitivity to distractions around them. An offer to show them something individually will lead to better productivity.

60

Direct communication methods are most effective.

Most people with autism communicate best in writing, according to Gardner. She suggests that supervisors write out very clear and direct instructions, whether in a job description, an assignment, or a performance appraisal. Spell out the specific desired behavior, such as, "Be ready to start working at exactly 9:00," rather than "Don't be late."

61

Allowing extra adjustment time is crucial.

Whether it is a change in location, routine, responsibilities or reporting, a person with autism usually needs at least twice as much time as his peers to get used to the difference, because of the extra emotions to process, according to Duncan. He will still perform his job as usual, but he may take longer to adjust and need to discuss the changes more than other employees.

Accommodations that can Help Autistic Employees

62

After hiring is best disclosure time.

The only way to receive job accommodations is to disclose the disability to the appropriate people, usually the HR manager and supervisor. For an employee with autism, meeting everyday demands without accommodations can be difficult to impossible, so disclosure of autism once hired is highly recommended.

63

Coaching can yield support and strategies.

PROVAIL is a coaching company that uses a team approach, involving companies, the applicant's family and others to learn as much as possible about the employee and the working environment. Job coaches should be thoughtful and observe and get to know the potential employee's strengths and work pace to help match him with the right job, said Goodwill.

64

Coaching can also help at work.

A job coach can stay involved indefinitely once someone is hired, and can be there as much as needed to advocate, create task lists and schedules, and communicate with both employee and employer to address any issues, said Goodwill. Because job coaches also help place employees, they often will already have a relationship with the employer.

65

Behind-the-scenes coaching is valuable.

For employees with autism, coaches can help even if they are not working with the employee on the job site. They can meet regularly on- or off-site to check in, even when things are going fine, according to Duncan. Regular coach-employee meetings ward off potential problems or misunderstandings, and the coach can ask questions regularly to make sure all is going well.

Benefits of Hiring People with Autism

66

Autistic employees' passions lead to productivity.

Because autistic individuals usually have intense, specific interests, the best jobs are those that allow them to be involved with those interests. For example, Gardner once had a job in sales. Selling isn't normally a strength in an autistic person, but because she was passionate about the product, she enjoyed the job and was very successful at it.

67

Strong interests make them work hard.

Hiring an autistic employee who is perfectly suited to the job because of an intense, passionate interest results in a win-win situation because when someone works on something he enjoys and has extensive knowledge in, he will "leap tall buildings," Gardner says, and be "one of the most productive people you would ever want to meet."

68

They love to be on time.

Like many people with autism, our son Trevor was always very aware of time, and wanted to stick to a schedule. He owned and used a watch from preschool on, and that attention to timeliness helped him when he had a job. Because autistic individuals thrive on routine, schedules, and predictability, they will rarely, if ever, be late to work or meetings, which is a dream for employers.

69

They work when nobody is watching.

When Trevor worked in maintenance for a church, we often received comments from his coworkers who had seen him doing heavy landscape work outside in the heat. Trevor didn't know anyone saw him, but he nevertheless worked hard when alone, never slacking or resting. It was that focus and commitment to do whatever he was asked that made him a model employee.

70

They find comfort in daily routines.

Trevor's supervisor referred to the routine of locking up every door in the building as Trevor's "security blanket." Autistic employees will perform well with tasks that involve routine and repetition, which are easy and comforting to them. Trevor also said the comfort of a routine helped him endure the other demands of the job.

71

They can be the most reliable.

Trevor's supervisor told him he was his "right-hand man." He said Trevor was more reliable than many of his other employees, and he could always count on him to do his work. He took literally no supervision, and he didn't have to check up on him. "As a supervisor, that's huge," Seidler said.

72

Autistic people have strong intrinsic motivation.

Trevor says that whenever he was told to do something at work, he just did it. When working in the kitchen at a summer camp, his fear of possible negative consequences, a typical trait for autistic individuals, actually motivated him to do his best. His supervisor was impressed with his commitment and that he finished his tasks so quickly.

73

Intense focus comes naturally to them.

Autistic people's intensity can be an asset that helps them focus on the task at hand. Trevor's extreme focusing ability allowed him to wash huge piles of dishes quickly without stopping or complaining. His kitchen supervisor remarked that Trevor was "like a machine" and couldn't believe how hard and fast he worked. Trevor said the repetition was comforting to him and he "just plowed right through it."

Be Aware of Unique Autistic Traits

74

Training should be given about autism.

The more training and education that takes place for managers and supervisors regarding how autistic individuals are wired, the better the work environment will be for everyone, according to Hilbert. Managers can have a big impact on acceptance among all employees by teaching awareness of the characteristics of autism, which will lead to better teamwork and productivity.

75

Autistic individuals can bring enormous creativity.

Workers with autism can have imaginations that are well above average. Managers should take advantage of this when looking for creative ideas or new ways to solve problems. If they give autistic team members opportunities to share their ideas, those ideas can lead to brilliant new concepts.

76

Autistic individuals need more processing time.

Because of so many things happening in their minds, those with autism find it difficult to verbalize with the same speed and clarity as others. They need coworkers and managers to give them a little extra time to explain and share their thoughts, and it will be worth the wait.

77

Emotions can be extreme at times.

A common fear of employers is that autistic employees don't have good emotional regulation. However, Gardner has found that a high percentage of those on the spectrum are calmer than the average employee. The difference is that when upset, an autistic person will show it more. However, they are also more energetic, enthusiastic, and productive.

78

Multi-tasking is not their friend.

While multi-tasking is a common phenomenon today, Trevor notes that autistic people have such intense focus that they work better when focusing on one thing at a time, and being able to either finish a task or come to a good stopping point, rather than going back and forth between two or more tasks. They can be more productive if allowed to work this way.

79

Switching tasks can be very challenging.

Quickly switching tasks is especially difficult for people with autism, especially when it is demanded of them with no notice. This is sometimes unavoidable, but if everyone would consider this a common courtesy—to give notice of a change when possible—the environment would be better for all in the workplace.

80

Interruptions can be hard to handle.

Employers and coworkers should note that people with autism generally don't like to be interrupted, whether it involves giving work responsibilities or making idle chitchat. Trevor didn't usually want to stop his work and make conversation with a coworker, because he felt like he was there only to work and was very focused on that.

81

They need notice about working late.

While autistic people are very good about being on time, they also have more difficulty than others with unexpected overtime work. Exercising courtesy by providing notification as early as possible that there might be a need to stay late will give them time to process the idea and accept it better. This would be appreciated by any employee.

82

Autistic individuals prefer a calm demeanor.

A supervisor who gives orders loudly or abruptly, interrupting the person's task at hand, is especially difficult for people with autism to handle. Trevor said that people like that stressed him out a lot, and he would handle the instructions much better if they were given in a softer tone, without interrupting, when possible.

83

Being blunt is part of autism.

Because of the extra time needed to sort out what they need to say, along with their black and white, literal thinking, autistic people tend to make comments that come out blunt, rude, or simply unusual. Others in the workplace should give them some grace and keep in mind that they don't mean to be rude.

84

Autistic employees can be literal thinkers.

Taking things literally is common with autistic people, and it can lead to misunderstandings. Supervisors should keep this in mind when communicating. Trevor was sometimes taken advantage of and teased by other employees because they found it funny when he took their sarcastic comments seriously.

85

Extra time is needed when new.

Starting a new job is more difficult for autistic people, because anything new and unfamiliar takes them more time and effort to get used to. They need extra time and patience to get the hang of the routine, environment, job duties, and coworkers, and will be working harder than the average employee to adjust.

86

Seeking help is difficult for them.

Some autistic people, including Trevor, tend to be very independent and don't like to ask for help with things they don't understand. It's very important that autistic employees develop the skill of asking for assistance or information while on the job. Supervisors and job coaches can make this easier by checking in and asking if the employee understands his work requirements.

87

Facial expressions can sometimes be deceiving.

People with autism usually have a harder time picking up meanings that are communicated by facial expressions, according to Duncan. Using clear and direct words helps them know what is meant. At the same time, they may not use appropriate facial expressions when they are talking. Asking for clarification is the best way to avoid miscommunication.

88

Face blindness is offensive to some.

Face blindness is the inability to recognize people by their faces at times, especially if they are in a different context, or are dressed differently. This common trait of people with autism can come across as rudeness or forgetfulness, so educating others about face blindness will help alleviate misunderstandings.

89

Social events can be hard work.

While social or morale events in the workplace are a "break" from work for typical workers, they can be hard work for those with autism, Hilbert said. They are often unstructured, and there is an expectation to make small talk. Plus, those with autism don't know what to expect and might feel anxiety about deviating from their routine and possibly falling behind in their planned work duties.

90

Giving advanced notice helps alleviate stress.

The more notice given, the better. Instead of saying, "Hey, it's Jane's birthday, we're all having cake in the break room right now!" the person with autism would prefer to know as soon as possible before the event, even if it's only 30 minutes, so he can finish what he is doing and prepare for the change in routine.

91

Learning about social skills benefits all.

Coworkers can learn to be patient and make an effort to give autistic employees some leeway in social skills that might be lacking. In an ideal workplace, everyone would be treated this way, regardless of whether or not a disability is known. Duncan suggests that employees try to not take things the wrong way, such as when employees with autism decline outings or social gatherings.

Social Expectations for Workers with Autism

92

Learning about social expectations breeds success.

Employees with autism should take it upon themselves to learn as much as possible about workplace social rules, which others pick up on without much effort. There are numerous books that address these situations in detail, such as break room behavior, lunchtimes, morale events, and any events outside of job duties.

93

Taking short breaks can reduce stress.

Autistic individuals can learn to be in tune with their own unique needs and stressors, and be prepared to do what it takes to still be effective on the job when stressful times happen, says Duncan. This could mean going to the car, taking a break, walking around the building, or whatever helps to de-stress, think, or cool off.

94

Allow time for friendships to grow.

Trevor's supervisor was open to learning about Trevor's needs due to his autism, but Seidler said, "Many people simply don't understand how to interact with people who have autism, and need extra time to build friendships." Autistic people should learn to be patient with other people, and allow time for good working relationships and friendships to develop.

95

Staying clean and groomed is vital.

Following basic hygiene and cleanliness is extremely important for being accepted in the workplace. Although Steve Jobs and others have been successful with odd hygiene habits, it is more likely to be a hindrance to success for an autistic person who already has some differences and challenges at work. Job coaches and books can help in this area.

96

Wear suitable clothing on the job.

Most workplaces have some type of dress code, even if it is unwritten. Learning and following these codes is essential. Employees can also learn by observing other employees, especially those at the same level, to see how closely they follow the rules. Oftentimes dress codes are simply guidelines, and are bent by employees, so violations need not be pointed out.

97

Courtesies and friendly exchanges are protocol.

While greetings are not often important to people with autism, they are an integral part of most jobs. Employees with autism must express basic greetings, such as "Hi," and "How are you?" with coworkers and customers, say "Thank-you," "Please," and "Excuse me," when appropriate, and show respect and courtesy to those around them in the workplace.

98

Small talk is expected at work.

"Professional small talk" (non-work related conversations within the workplace) has appropriate times and places. It is important to learn what to say and how long to continue the conversations among coworkers. Learning body language and other cues will also help the employee fit in to the workday culture. Books and job coaching can help improve these skills.

99

Every workplace has its unique language.

All companies have special terms that refer to anything from departments to job titles. Acronyms are especially prevalent, and even everyday slang and cliches are already challenging for those with autism. Many companies have handouts with acronyms and buzzwords defined. The autistic worker should realize that most new workers are also not comfortable with all terminology, but learning will come in time.

100

Keep searching for the perfect fit.

In closing, please don't give up on finding a job or career that fits you perfectly. There are so many ways to get help and a number of helpful methods for landing meaningful employment. Some positions won't work out, so try to learn from them, review and adjust your strategies, and try again. I wish you a productive career and a fulfilling life of independence and making a difference in the workplace and in the world.

Sources Cited

Elaine Duncan, MA, LMHC
Psychotherapist in Autism & EDMR Specialist
Counselingredmond.com

Sara Gardner
Program Manager, Autism Spectrum Navigators
Bellevue College
Bellevuecollege.edu/autismspectrumnavigators

Michael Goodwill
Manager of Transition Services
PROVAIL
Provail.org

Lisa Iland Hilbert, MS
Owner of Social Bridge, LLC
Socialbridgeseattle.com

Jeri Kendle
Social Enterprise Strategist
Southwest Autism Research & Resource Center
Autismcenter.org

Kim Kimbell
Human Resources Consultant

Michael Maloney
Executive Director
Organization for Autism Research
ResearchAutism.org

Sources Cited, continued

Paige Morrow
Extraordinary Ventures
Extraordinaryventures.org

Manfred Seidler
Plant Engineer, Crossroads Bible Church

Garry Burge and Ben Wilshire, Adult Asperger's and Autism Advocates
GarryBurge.com

U.S. Department of Labor, public domain, dol.gov.

Najarian, Tamar, "34 Best and 10 Worst Jobs for Adults with Autism" emaxhealth.com.

Danya International (danya.com), Southwest Autism Research & Resource Center (autismcenter.org) and Organization for Autism Research, Mike Maloney, Executive Director, (researchautism.org) *Life Journey Through Autism: A Guide for Transition to Adulthood* (2008)

Roux, Ann M., Shattuck, Paul T., Cooper, Benjamin P., Anderson, Kristy, et al. "Postsecondary Employment Experiences Among Young Adults with an Autism Spectrum Disorder," *Journal of the American Academy of Child & Adolescent Psychiatry*, Volume 52, Issue 9, (2013) 931-939.

For Further Reading and Information

Social Thinking at Work: Why Should I Care? by Michelle Garcia Winner

The Hidden Curriculum: Practical Solutions for Understanding Unstated Rules in Social Situations by Brenda Smith Myles

The Unwritten Rules of Social Relationships: Decoding Social Mysteries through the Unique Perspectives of Autism by Temple Grandin

Six-Word Lessons on Growing Up Autistic by Trevor Pacelli

Six-Word Lessons for Dads with Autistic Kids by Lonnie Pacelli

The Kindergarten Adventures of Amazing Grace by Briana Pacelli

For more resources on autism, go to
GrowingUpAutistic.com

About the *Six-Word Lessons Series*

Legend has it that Ernest Hemingway was challenged to write a story using only six words. He responded with the story, "For sale: baby shoes, never worn." The story tickles the imagination. Why were the shoes never worn? The answers are left up to the reader's imagination.

This style of writing has a number of aliases: postcard fiction, flash fiction, and micro fiction. Lonnie Pacelli was introduced to this concept in 2009 by a friend, and started thinking about how this extreme brevity could apply to today's communication culture of text messages, tweets and Facebook posts. He wrote the first book, *Six-Word Lessons for Project Managers*, then started helping other authors write and publish their own books in the series.

The books all have six-word chapters with six-word lesson titles, each followed by a one-page description. They can be written by entrepreneurs who want to promote their businesses, or anyone with a message to share.

See the entire *Six-Word Lessons Series* at 6wordlessons.com

32006973R00073

Made in the USA
San Bernardino, CA
25 March 2016